The Scrum Master's Handbook: Practical Tips for Agile Excellence

Published in December 2023.

About the Author
Abdullah Oguz, Ph.D., PMP®

Currently, an Assistant Professor of Management Information Systems at Central Connecticut State University, Dr. Abdullah Oguz is a seasoned academic and project management professional. He holds a Ph.D. in Information Systems from the University of North Carolina at Greensboro, where his research focused on "Cyberbullying in Global Virtual Teams."

Dr. Oguz's extensive research and teaching career have led him to develop expertise in areas like workplace cyberbullying, global virtual teams, artificial intelligence, and agile project management. He has authored the book "Project Management: Navigating the Complexity with a Systematic Approach," which has been widely adopted in project management courses across various universities.

With a rich background in project management, Dr. Oguz has managed substantial EU-funded projects, focusing on capacity building and the implementation of cutting-edge IT and security systems during his tenure as a Project Management Professional in the Turkish Customs Enforcement administration. He holds the esteemed PMP® credential, demonstrating his commitment to the field of project management.

In the realm of academia, Dr. Oguz has been instrumental in proposing and establishing an AI Lab at CCSU, signifying his forward-thinking approach toward education and research. His teaching repertoire spans various subjects, including agile project management, business analytics, programming with Python, and systems analysis and design, reflecting his diverse expertise in information systems.

Dr. Oguz's commitment to his field is further highlighted by his active involvement in professional organizations like the Project Management Institute (PMI) and the Association for Information Systems (AIS). He is also a respected figure in the academic community, with numerous publications in prestigious journals and contributions to international conferences.

As an author, educator, and practitioner, Dr. Abdullah Oguz brings a wealth of knowledge and experience to the field of Agile project management, making him a valuable guide for anyone looking to navigate this dynamic and challenging arena.

Table of Contents

Introduction

The Scrum Master plays a crucial role in the implementation and success of Scrum within a team. As defined in "The Scrum Guide - The Definitive Guide to Scrum: The Rules of the Game" authored by Ken Schwaber and Jeff Sutherland in 2020, and explained by various Agile sources, the primary responsibilities of a Scrum Master include:

1. **Promoting and Supporting Scrum**: The Scrum Master is responsible for ensuring that the team understands and implements Scrum theory, practices, rules, and values. This involves helping everyone in the organization grasp the nuances of Scrum and guiding them in mastering its application.

2. **Coaching Team Members**: A key responsibility of a Scrum Master as a servant leader is to coach team members, ensuring they are well-trained and understand Agile values, principles, and the various Scrum events and artifacts. The Scrum Master also ensures that team members are aware of their accountabilities within the Agile framework.

3. **Facilitating Team Effectiveness**: The Scrum Master works to keep the team operating effectively within the Scrum values. This involves planning and leading meetings, keeping the team on track, and addressing any obstacles that might impede the team's progress.

4. **Clearing Obstacles and Establishing an Effective Environment**: Part of the role involves clearing any hindrances to the team's progress and establishing an environment conducive to effective and efficient work. This also includes addressing team dynamics and ensuring a harmonious and productive team atmosphere.

Importance of Understanding What Not to Do

Understanding the role of a Scrum Master also involves recognizing what not to do. Missteps or misinterpretations of the role can lead to inefficiencies and diminish the effectiveness of the Scrum framework within a team. This book focuses on highlighting these potential pitfalls by guiding how to avoid them.

Focus on Practical, Concise Advice

"The Scrum Master's Handbook: Practical Tips for Agile Excellence" is designed to offer direct and practical advice. Each section presents clear, concise guidance to help new Scrum Masters navigate their roles successfully. The book aims to distill complex concepts into easily digestible tips and strategies, making it an ideal resource for those new to the Scrum Master role or looking to refine their approach.

In summary, this book serves as a comprehensive guide for new Scrum Masters, offering insights into the essential aspects of the role, while also cautioning against common mistakes. By focusing on practical, actionable advice, it aims to equip Scrum Masters with the knowledge and tools needed for success in this dynamic and critical role in Agile project management.

Advice 1: "Avoid Acting as the Product Owner"

Key Insights: The Importance of Role Clarity in Agile Teams

In my research and teaching in the field of project management, I've consistently emphasized the significance of clear roles within project teams including the Agile teams. The distinction between the Scrum Master and the Product Owner is particularly crucial. I've observed in case studies and industry practices how the blending of these roles can lead to confusion and inefficiency. It's akin to mixing the roles of a director and an actor in a play – each is vital, but they have distinct responsibilities.

Understanding Each Role

- **Product Owner Responsibilities**: The Product Owner is the strategist, defining the product vision and managing the backlog. They ensure that the team's efforts align with business objectives, acting as a conduit between stakeholders and the development team.

- **Scrum Master Role**: The Scrum Master's role is focused on facilitating the Scrum process, supporting the team's use of Scrum, removing impediments, and ensuring efficiency. As a servant-leader, the Scrum Master helps the team self-organize and collaborate effectively.

Practical Tips

1. **Foster Open Communication**: Regularly engage in discussions about roles and responsibilities with the Product Owner and the team.

   - *Example*: Schedule monthly alignment meetings where the Scrum Master, Product Owner, and team members clarify their roles, responsibilities, and expectations to ensure everyone is on the same page and to prevent any role overlap.

2. **Respect the Backlog**: Steer clear of directly influencing the product backlog and focus on supporting the team in understanding and executing backlog items as outlined by the Product Owner.

   - *Example*: During sprint planning, let the Product Owner present and prioritize backlog items, while you facilitate the team's understanding and breakdown of these items into actionable tasks.

3. **Facilitate, Don't Dictate**: Shift your focus in meetings to facilitating discussions, allowing the Product Owner to lead product-related decision-making.

   - *Example*: In backlog refinement meetings, encourage open discussion and questions about backlog items but refrain from giving directives, letting the Product Owner provide the necessary clarity and direction.

4. **Educate the Team**: Make sure the team has a clear understanding of the distinct roles of the Scrum Master and the Product Owner.

   - *Example*: Organize a workshop or a team session specifically dedicated to discussing the different roles in Scrum, their responsibilities, and how they complement each other, ensuring everyone understands the unique functions and boundaries of each role.

5. **Reflect on Your Role Regularly**: Periodically assess your actions to ensure they are aligned with the Scrum Master's role of facilitation rather than encroaching upon the responsibilities of the Product Owner.

   - *Example*: Keep a personal log or journal to reflect on your daily or weekly actions, evaluating whether they align with facilitating and supporting the team, and adjust your approach as needed to stay true to the Scrum Master's role.

The effective segregation of the Scrum Master and Product Owner roles is a cornerstone of productive Agile environments. By adhering to these guidelines, a Scrum Master can effectively navigate the nuances of their role, avoiding pitfalls associated with role confusion. This clarity ensures a more harmonious and productive Agile environment, with each role contributing effectively to the team's success.

Advice 2: "Do Not Take Over Self-Organizing Team Responsibilities"

Key Insights: Empowering Self-Organizing Teams

The essence of Agile and Scrum lies in the empowerment of self-organizing teams. Such teams, when provided with the right environment and trust, can effectively manage their work and make decisions. However, when a Scrum Master takes over responsibilities that belong to the team, it can impede their autonomy, hinder their development, and affect their motivation and productivity.

Understanding the Essence of Self-Organization

- **Trust and Empowerment**: Trusting the team's ability to manage their work is a fundamental aspect of Agile methodologies. This trust fosters a sense of ownership and responsibility among team members.

- **Facilitation Over Dictation**: The Scrum Master's role is to facilitate and guide, not to control or micromanage. This distinction is critical in nurturing a self-organizing team.

- **Learning Through Experience**: Encourage the team to learn from their experiences, including their mistakes. This approach is vital for team growth and development.

Practical Tips

1. **Guide, Don't Control**: Offer guidance to the team as needed, while refraining from controlling or dictating their work.

   - *Example*: In project meetings, rather than assigning tasks, ask team members to volunteer for tasks based on their strengths and interests. Provide your insights and suggestions only when asked or when absolutely necessary.

2. **Encourage Decision-Making**: Create an environment where the team feels empowered and motivated to make their own decisions.

   - *Example*: During planning sessions, instead of presenting a predefined plan, encourage the team to brainstorm and come up with their own strategies and solutions, offering your support and facilitation to keep the process on track.

3. **Provide Necessary Tools and Resources**: Make sure the team has access to the required tools and resources for effective self-organization.

- *Example*: Facilitate a session to identify any gaps in tools or resources, such as software for task management or platforms for communication, and work towards providing these essentials to the team.

4. **Champion Reflective Practices**: Regularly engage in retrospectives to allow the team to reflect, learn, and evolve.

   - *Example*: Conduct end-of-sprint retrospectives where the team can discuss what went well, what didn't, and collaboratively find ways to improve. Encourage open and honest feedback without leading the conversation.

5. **Recognize and Celebrate Autonomy**: Celebrate the instances where the team successfully self-organizes, reinforcing the importance of autonomy.

   - *Example*: Acknowledge and highlight specific instances where the team took initiative and made decisions independently, either in team meetings or through internal communications, to showcase and celebrate these successes.

By adhering to these practices, a Scrum Master can cultivate a truly self-organizing team. Such a team not only manages its own work effectively but also aligns closely with the core principles of autonomy and empowerment central to Agile methodologies.

Advice 3: "Do Not Behave Like a Traditional Project Manager"

Key Insights: Agile vs. Traditional Project Management

Transitioning from traditional project management to Scrum involves a profound shift in mindset and methodology. Traditional project management typically adheres to a linear, structured approach, while Scrum champions an iterative, flexible process focused on collaboration and adaptability. For Scrum Masters, fully embracing these differences is crucial for nurturing the dynamism and responsiveness that are the hallmarks of successful Agile teams.

Understanding the Scrum Approach

- **Flexibility Over Rigidity**: Scrum prioritizes flexibility and responsiveness to change, in stark contrast to the fixed, rigid planning often seen in traditional project management.

- **Collaboration and Empowerment**: Unlike the top-down decision-making of traditional methods, Scrum focuses on empowering teams to collaborate and make decisions.

- **Iterative Progress**: Scrum breaks the project into manageable iterations, allowing for regular feedback and continual adaptation, a significant departure from traditional project management's linear progression.

Practical Tips

1. **Foster a Collaborative Environment**: Create a space where open communication is the norm, and every team member feels comfortable sharing their ideas and opinions.

   - *Example*: During team meetings, encourage each member to contribute their thoughts on project decisions. Facilitate discussions that allow for diverse viewpoints, ensuring that quieter team members also have the opportunity to speak up.

2. **Embrace Change and Adaptability**: Demonstrate a willingness to adapt to changing project scopes and requirements, embodying the Agile value of flexibility.

   - *Example*: When project requirements shift, lead a team discussion to collaboratively assess the changes and adapt the plan. Show openness to new ideas and approaches, even if they deviate from the original plan.

3. **Focus on Value Delivery**: Redirect the team's focus from merely completing tasks to delivering real value aligned with project goals.

   - *Example*: In sprint planning sessions, instead of just ticking off tasks, discuss how each task contributes to the overall project objectives. Help the team prioritize work based on value delivery rather than just task completion.

4. **Encourage Team Autonomy**: Support the team in self-managing and making decisions independently, stepping back from a directive role.

   - *Example*: Allow the team to lead sprint planning and task estimation. Offer guidance only when asked, and trust the team's ability to manage their workload and make effective decisions.

5. **Promote Continuous Improvement**: Regularly involve the team in retrospectives to reflect on processes and identify areas for improvement.

   - *Example*: Conduct end-of-sprint retrospectives focusing not just on what was achieved, but also on how processes can be refined. Encourage each team member to suggest one area for improvement and one area of strength, fostering a culture of continuous growth.

By embracing these Agile principles and practices, Scrum Masters can effectively transition from traditional project management methods to those aligning with Scrum. This shift is vital for creating an environment where Agile teams can not only thrive but also deliver their maximum potential, staying responsive and adaptive in a dynamic project landscape.

Advice 4: "Embrace Servant Leadership"

Key Insights: The Essence of Servant Leadership in Scrum

Servant leadership, a core component of the Scrum Master role, distinctly sets it apart from traditional leadership roles. This approach emphasizes support and empowerment over direction and control. As a servant leader, the Scrum Master prioritizes the team's needs, fostering their growth and acting as a catalyst for success. In my experience, adopting servant leadership has been transformative, not only in guiding teams but also in building a culture of trust, collaboration, and productivity.

Understanding Servant Leadership

- **Empowerment Over Authority**: True servant leadership is about empowering the team, not asserting authority. It's about creating opportunities for team success and helping them navigate challenges.

- **Focus on Team Needs**: It's crucial to understand and meet the needs of team members. This could involve providing resources, removing obstacles, or giving support and guidance.

- **Creating a Supportive Environment**: A servant leader's goal is to cultivate an environment conducive to growth, learning, and teamwork.

Practical Tips

1. **Listen Actively**: Prioritize listening to your team's feedback, ideas, and concerns with full attention and openness.

   - *Example*: In team meetings, practice reflective listening by paraphrasing or summarizing what team members say, showing that their input is heard and valued. This approach encourages deeper understanding and builds trust within the team.

2. **Encourage and Support**: Act as a source of encouragement and support for your team, helping them navigate both successes and challenges.

- *Example*: When a team member achieves a milestone or overcomes a difficult challenge, publicly acknowledge their effort and success. Similarly, offer constructive support and guidance when they face obstacles, helping them to learn and grow from the experience.

3. **Facilitate, Don't Impose**: Guide team discussions and decision-making processes without imposing your views or solutions.

   - *Example*: During sprint planning or problem-solving sessions, ask open-ended questions to stimulate thinking and exploration of ideas. Allow the team to arrive at decisions collectively, rather than steering them towards a preconceived solution.

4. **Be Approachable and Available**: Ensure that you are accessible and approachable to your team members, fostering a culture of open communication and trust.

   - *Example*: Keep your virtual or physical door open for team members to discuss their ideas, concerns, or seek guidance. Regularly check in with team members individually to offer your support and establish a rapport.

5. **Lead by Example**: Demonstrate Agile and Scrum values in your daily actions and interactions, setting a positive example for your team.

   - *Example*: Show commitment to Agile principles in how you manage your own tasks and interactions with the team and stakeholders. For instance, exhibit flexibility in adapting to changes and show respect and empathy in all communications.

By embracing servant leadership, a Scrum Master can effectively guide their team through the complexities of Agile projects, fostering an environment of growth, collaboration, and continuous improvement. This leadership style is instrumental in building high-performing teams that are self-motivated, cohesive, and aligned with Agile values.

Advice 5: "Cultivate High-Quality Communication"

Key Insights: The Importance of Communication in Scrum

Effective communication is the backbone of any successful Scrum team. As a Scrum Master, facilitating high-quality communication within the team, as well as between the team and external stakeholders, is crucial. It's not just about ensuring information is exchanged; it's about fostering an environment where communication is clear, transparent, and constructive, enhancing collaboration and understanding.

Understanding High-Quality Communication

- **Clarity and Transparency**: Communication should be clear and transparent, avoiding misunderstandings and ensuring that everyone is on the same page.

- **Inclusiveness**: Ensuring that all team members, regardless of their role or level of experience, have the opportunity to voice their opinions and concerns.

- **Feedback and Adaptation**: Encouraging a culture of constructive feedback, where team members feel comfortable both giving and receiving input for continuous improvement.

Practical Tips

1. **Facilitate Open Dialogues**: Encourage team members to share their thoughts, ideas, and concerns through open discussions.

   - *Example*: Initiate regular team huddles or open forums where project updates, creative ideas, and any concerns can be openly discussed. These sessions should be in a supportive environment where every team member feels comfortable and valued.

2. **Promote Active Listening**: Active listening is crucial and involves full concentration, understanding, responding, and remembering what is said.

   - *Example*: In meetings, actively listen and then succinctly summarize the points raised by team members. This practice not only confirms understanding but also encourages others to listen actively and engage in meaningful dialogue.

3. **Use Various Communication Channels**: Effectively use different modes of communication, recognizing each one's strengths and limitations.

   - *Example*: Reserve face-to-face meetings for complex, nuanced discussions; utilize chat tools for quick, day-to-day communications; and leverage virtual meetings for coordinating with remote team members, ensuring each medium is used in the most effective context.

4. **Encourage Regular Feedback**: Regular feedback is essential for continuous improvement and should be ingrained in the team's culture.

   - *Example*: Conduct feedback sessions at the end of each sprint for collective reflection and arrange one-on-one meetings to discuss individual progress and challenges, thereby fostering a culture of continuous feedback and personal growth.

5. **Model Effective Communication**: Demonstrate clear, respectful, and effective communication in your interactions.

   - *Example*: Consistently communicate with clarity and respect, especially in conflict resolutions. Show how to address disagreements with empathy and assertiveness, setting a standard for the team.

6. **Address Communication Barriers**: Actively identify and mitigate barriers to effective communication, whether technological, cultural, or interpersonal.

- *Example*: Utilize translation tools or provide documents in multiple languages to overcome language barriers. Conduct workshops or discussions to enhance understanding and navigate cultural differences, strengthening cross-cultural communication within the team.

By cultivating high-quality communication, a Scrum Master can significantly enhance team dynamics, collaboration, and overall project success. This involves not only facilitating the exchange of information but also nurturing an environment where communication contributes positively to the team's workflow and Agile practices.

Advice 6: "Master the Art of Removing Impediments"

Key Insights: The Scrum Master's Role in Impediment Removal

One of the primary responsibilities of a Scrum Master is to identify and remove impediments that hinder the team's progress. Impediments can range from organizational obstacles to technical challenges or interpersonal issues. Efficiently addressing these barriers is crucial for maintaining the momentum of the Agile team and ensuring smooth sprint execution.

Understanding Impediment Removal

- **Proactive Identification**: Being proactive in identifying potential impediments even before they impact the team.

- **Empowerment and Support**: While removing impediments, also focus on empowering the team to overcome obstacles independently in the future.

- **Varied Nature of Impediments**: Recognize that impediments can be diverse, including technical, process-related, organizational, or interpersonal challenges.

Practical Tips

1. **Maintain Open Communication**: Foster an environment where team members feel comfortable sharing their challenges.

   - *Example*: Create a dedicated space or time during stand-up meetings for team members to flag any potential impediments. This practice encourages early identification and prompt action.

2. **Prioritize Impediments**: Assess and prioritize impediments based on their impact on the team's progress.

   - *Example*: Use a simple categorization system (e.g., high, medium, low impact) during team discussions to prioritize which impediments to address first, ensuring that the most critical issues are tackled promptly.

3. **Collaborate on Solutions**: Work together with the team to find and implement solutions to impediments.

   - *Example*: Organize brainstorming sessions where team members can suggest and discuss possible solutions. This approach not only fosters team collaboration but also often leads to more innovative and effective resolutions.

4. **Leverage Networks and Resources**: Utilize internal and external networks and resources for solving complex impediments.

   - *Example*: Reach out to other Scrum Masters, department heads, or external experts for advice or assistance in resolving specific technical or organizational challenges that the team cannot address alone.

5. **Track and Follow Up**: Keep a log of impediments and their resolutions, and ensure ongoing issues are being resolved.

   - *Example*: Maintain an impediment log in your team's shared space and regularly review the status of each issue in sprint retrospectives, ensuring that no impediment is overlooked or left unresolved.

6. **Educate the Team**: Use resolved impediments as learning opportunities to prevent similar issues in the future.

   - *Example*: Discuss how each resolved impediment was addressed during retrospectives and explore how similar future challenges can be avoided or mitigated, turning challenges into learning opportunities for the whole team.

By mastering the art of removing impediments, a Scrum Master not only ensures the smooth functioning of the current sprint but also contributes to the long-term efficiency and effectiveness of the team. This role is pivotal in fostering a productive and unobstructed Agile working environment.

Advice 7: "Facilitate Effective Sprint Planning"

Key Insights: The Criticality of Sprint Planning in Scrum

Sprint planning is a fundamental ceremony in Scrum that sets the tone for the entire sprint. As a Scrum Master, facilitating an effective sprint planning session is crucial. This meeting determines what will be delivered in the sprint and lays out the plan for achieving it. Poorly executed sprint planning can lead to confusion, unrealistic commitments, and a lack of clarity on goals and priorities, ultimately affecting the sprint's success.

Understanding Sprint Planning

- **Realistic Goal Setting**: Ensuring that the goals set during sprint planning are achievable and aligned with the team's capacity and the product backlog.

- **Team Collaboration**: Sprint planning is a collaborative effort involving the entire team, including the Product Owner.

- **Clarity and Commitment**: The team should leave the meeting with a clear understanding of what needs to be done and a commitment to the sprint goal.

Practical Tips

1. **Prepare in Advance**: Collaborate with the Product Owner to groom the backlog effectively before the sprint planning session.

    - *Example*: Schedule a pre-planning meeting with the Product Owner to review and prioritize the backlog items, ensuring that the high-priority tasks are well-defined and ready for team discussion.

2. **Facilitate, Don't Dictate**: Guide the sprint planning discussion, ensuring it remains focused and productive, while allowing the team and Product Owner to lead the conversation about achievable goals.

    - *Example*: Use open-ended questions to steer the discussion and help the team explore various options for achieving sprint goals, rather than prescribing specific tasks or solutions.

3. **Ensure Clarity on Sprint Goals**: Make the sprint goals clear and ensure every team member understands and agrees on what needs to be accomplished.

    - *Example*: Begin the sprint planning session by clearly stating the sprint goals and checking with each team member to confirm their understanding and agreement.

4. **Manage Time Effectively**: Adhere to the timebox of the sprint planning meeting and prioritize discussion topics to cover the most critical aspects efficiently.

    - *Example*: Use a timer to keep track of time during the sprint planning session and ensure that discussions do not overrun, focusing on the essential agenda items.

5. **Encourage Team Input**: Actively involve each team member in the planning process, especially in task estimation and commitment.

   - *Example*: Encourage every team member to voice their opinions on task estimations and resource allocation, ensuring a collaborative approach to committing to sprint tasks.

6. **Visualize the Sprint Plan**: Utilize visual tools or a physical board to outline the sprint backlog and demonstrate how it aligns with the sprint goals.

   - *Example*: Use a Kanban board or digital project management tool to visually map out the sprint backlog, allowing the team to see how each item contributes to achieving the sprint objectives.

7. **Confirm Team Commitment**: Conclude the sprint planning session by ensuring that the team collectively commits to the sprint plan and understands their individual responsibilities.

   - *Example*: At the end of the session, go around the room and have each team member verbally confirm their commitment to the sprint tasks they are responsible for, fostering a sense of accountability and shared purpose.

By facilitating effective sprint planning, a Scrum Master helps the team set realistic and achievable goals for the sprint, ensuring a clear direction and a shared understanding of the tasks ahead. This is a critical step in paving the way for a successful and productive sprint.

Advice 8: "Effectively Manage Time-Boxing and Prevent Scope Creep"

Key Insights: The Importance of Time-Boxing in Scrum

In Scrum, time-boxing is a critical element that helps teams manage their time effectively and maintain focus. Sprints, along with other Scrum events like daily standups and retrospectives, are time-boxed to ensure efficiency and prompt delivery. As a Scrum Master, it's important to help the team understand and respect these time constraints to prevent scope creep and ensure successful completion of sprints.

Understanding Time-Boxing in Scrum

- **Fixed Duration**: Each sprint and Scrum event has a fixed duration, which should be adhered to promote discipline and focus.

- **Avoiding Scope Creep**: Scope creep occurs when new work is added to the sprint without corresponding adjustments. Managing this effectively is key to maintaining sprint goals.

- **Balancing Flexibility and Discipline**: While Agile values flexibility, discipline in time-boxing is essential for maintaining the structure and momentum of the project.

Practical Tips

1. **Clearly Define Sprint Goals**: Collaborate with the Product Owner and the team to set clear, achievable goals for each sprint.

   - *Example*: Initiate sprint planning sessions with a goal-setting phase where the Product Owner outlines the objectives, and the team aligns on what can realistically be achieved within the sprint timeframe.

2. **Educate the Team on Time-Boxing**: Ensure every team member understands the concept and importance of time-boxing in Scrum.

   - *Example*: Conduct a brief workshop or a discussion session at the beginning of a project to explain the concept of time-boxing, its role in Scrum, and how it contributes to the team's success.

3. **Enforce Time Limits in Scrum Ceremonies**: Adhere strictly to the time limits set for Scrum ceremonies like daily standups and retrospectives.

   - *Example*: Use a timer during Scrum ceremonies to ensure they start and end on time. For example, limit daily standups to 15 minutes and enforce this rule to maintain focus and efficiency.

4. **Monitor Sprint Progress**: Regularly track the progress of the sprint against its goals.

   - *Example*: Utilize burndown charts or similar tracking tools to monitor the team's progress in real-time, identifying any deviations from the plan early on.

5. **Address Scope Creep Proactively**: Actively manage any additional work requests during a sprint.

   - *Example*: If new tasks are proposed, discuss them with the Product Owner and the team to assess their impact on the sprint goals. Decide whether to incorporate, defer, or reject these additions based on their urgency and importance.

6. **Facilitate Efficient Meetings**: Ensure that meetings are focused and productive, with clear agendas.

   - *Example*: Prepare and distribute an agenda before each meeting, and during the meeting, keep the discussion on topic to ensure that all relevant points are covered within the allocated time.

7. **Encourage Team to Speak Up**: Empower team members to express concerns about time-boxing or scope creep.

   - *Example*: Create an open environment where team members feel comfortable raising concerns about overcommitment or deviations from the sprint plan, allowing for timely adjustments and discussions.

8. **Review and Adapt**: Continuously review and refine the approach to time-boxing and sprint planning.

- *Example*: Use sprint retrospectives as an opportunity to reflect on the effectiveness of time management and to gather team feedback on areas for improvement.

By effectively managing time-boxing and preventing scope creep, a Scrum Master ensures that the team stays focused and on track, leading to more successful sprint completions and overall project progress. This disciplined approach is essential for maintaining the integrity and efficiency of the Agile process.

Advice 9: "Define and Uphold the 'Definition of Done'"

Key Insights: Importance of 'Definition of Done' in Scrum

In Scrum, the 'Definition of Done' (DoD) is a crucial agreement that outlines the criteria required to consider a task or user story as complete. As a Scrum Master, it's important to facilitate the creation and maintenance of a clear and comprehensive DoD. This ensures consistency, quality, and a shared understanding among the team about what it means for work to be completed.

Understanding the 'Definition of Done'

- **Clarity and Transparency**: A well-defined DoD provides clarity and transparency, enabling the team to deliver work that meets expected quality standards.

- **Collaborative Agreement**: The DoD should be collaboratively agreed upon by the team and aligned with stakeholder expectations.

- **Continuous Review and Adaptation**: The DoD should be regularly revisited and adapted as necessary to reflect changes in project requirements or team capabilities.

Practical Tips

1. **Facilitate the Creation of the DoD**: Lead the team in collaboratively establishing the Definition of Done, ensuring clarity and measurability.

   - *Example*: Organize a dedicated session with the team to discuss and define what 'done' means for different types of tasks, ensuring that the criteria are specific, clear, and aligned with project goals.

2. **Ensure Team Buy-In**: Confirm that every team member understands and agrees with the DoD, as collective agreement is key to its successful application.

   - *Example*: After defining the DoD, have each team member explain it in their own words to ensure understanding and agreement, addressing any ambiguities or concerns that arise.

3. **Integrate DoD in Daily Work**: Encourage the team to consistently reference and apply the DoD in their daily tasks and decision-making.

   - *Example*: Incorporate reminders or checkpoints in daily standups or task boards where team members can confirm that their work meets the DoD before marking tasks as complete.

4. **Review DoD in Retrospectives**: Consistently reassess the DoD during retrospectives to ensure it remains relevant and effective.

   - *Example*: Allocate time in each retrospective to discuss the DoD's effectiveness and whether any aspects need to be updated based on recent experiences or project evolutions.

5. **Educate Stakeholders**: Explain the significance of the DoD to stakeholders and how it underpins the project's quality and success.

- *Example*: During stakeholder meetings, present the DoD and illustrate how it ensures quality and consistency in deliverables, aligning stakeholder expectations with the team's work process.

6. **Monitor and Enforce Compliance**: Regularly verify that completed work aligns with the established DoD, addressing discrepancies as they arise.

   - *Example*: Conduct periodic reviews of completed tasks or user stories to check their adherence to the DoD, and discuss any deviations in team meetings to prevent recurrence.

7. **Adapt the DoD as Needed**: Remain flexible to modifying the DoD in response to project changes or new insights about different work types.

   - *Example*: If new technologies or methodologies are introduced during the project, revisit the DoD with the team to ensure it still applies or if adjustments are needed to accommodate these changes.

By defining and upholding a clear 'Definition of Done,' a Scrum Master plays a vital role in ensuring that the team consistently delivers high-quality work that meets both internal standards and stakeholder expectations. This practice is fundamental in maintaining transparency, quality, and alignment within the Scrum framework.

Advice 10: "Do Not Lead the Daily Standups"
Key Insights: Facilitating Effective Standups
In Scrum, the daily standup is pivotal for synchronizing team efforts and planning daily work. The effectiveness of these meetings largely depends on them being team-led rather than led by the Scrum Master. As a facilitator, the Scrum Master's role is to ensure the standup remains focused, timely, and productive,

fostering an environment where team members take ownership and actively engage.

Understanding the Scrum Master's Facilitative Role

- **Facilitation Over Direction**: The Scrum Master should create an environment conducive to effective communication and collaboration, avoiding taking a directive role in the conversation.

- **Empowering Team Members**: Encourage team members to lead the standup, promoting a sense of ownership and responsibility for both their individual work and the project's progress.

- **Efficiency in Meetings**: Focus on making standups concise and goal-oriented, stepping in only to keep the discussion on track or address any deviations from the agenda.

Practical Tips

1. **Set Clear Expectations**: Make it known that the standup is a team-centric meeting and explain its objectives and structure.

   - *Example*: At the start of a sprint, clearly define the purpose of the daily standup to the team, emphasizing that it's a time for them to sync up on progress and challenges, not a status report to the Scrum Master.

2. **Rotate the Facilitator Role**: Empower team members by having them take turns facilitating the standup.

   - *Example*: Implement a rotation system where a different team member leads the standup each day or week. This approach encourages engagement and gives everyone a chance to develop their facilitation skills.

3. **Prompt Participation Without Dominating**: Use open-ended questions to encourage discussion among team members.

   - *Example*: Instead of directly asking for updates, pose questions like "What challenges are we facing today?" or

"How can we help each other move forward?" to stimulate interactive discussions.

4. **Intervene Only When Necessary**: Step in to steer the conversation back on course if it strays, but refrain from dominating the discussion.

   - *Example*: If the conversation veers off-topic, gently redirect it back to the main focus of the standup, but allow the team to continue leading the dialogue.

5. **Encourage Direct Peer Communication**: Create an environment where team members address each other, not just the Scrum Master.

   - *Example*: Encourage team members to speak directly to one another during the standup, especially when discussing interdependencies or seeking assistance, fostering a sense of team collaboration and direct communication.

By adopting these approaches, the Scrum Master ensures that daily standups effectively serve their purpose. These meetings become platforms for facilitating team coordination and communication, reinforcing the principles of team autonomy and collective responsibility essential in Scrum.

Advice 11: "Establish Effective Metrics for Tracking Scrum Team Progress"

Key Insights: The Role of Metrics in Scrum

In Scrum, measuring and tracking the team's progress is crucial for continuous improvement and informed decision-making. As a Scrum Master, it's your responsibility to help the team establish and utilize effective metrics and reporting practices. The right metrics not only provide insight into the team's performance but also highlight areas for improvement and help in aligning the team's efforts with the project goals.

Understanding the Importance of Metrics in Scrum

- **Transparency and Visibility**: Good metrics offer transparency and visibility into the team's work and progress.

- **Guiding Continuous Improvement**: Metrics can identify areas where the team can improve, driving the continuous improvement process.

- **Informed Decision-Making**: Data from metrics can guide the team and stakeholders in making informed decisions.

Practical Tips

1. **Choose Relevant Metrics**: Carefully select metrics that align with the team's goals and the project objectives.

   - *Example*: Implement metrics like velocity for measuring the amount of work completed in a sprint, and sprint burndown charts to track daily progress, ensuring they directly relate to the team's objectives and enhance understanding of project status.

2. **Avoid Vanity Metrics**: Focus on metrics that provide genuine insights into performance and value delivery, rather than those that merely look impressive.

   - *Example*: Steer clear of metrics that only measure busywork or sheer quantity without reflecting the quality or impact of the work done.

3. **Educate the Team on Metrics**: Ensure the team has a comprehensive understanding of each metric and its relevance to their work and project outcomes.

   - *Example*: Organize a training session or workshop to explain each metric, how it is calculated, and how it can be used to guide decision-making and process improvements.

4. **Use Metrics for Insight, Not Judgment**: Position metrics as a means for gaining insights and identifying areas for improvement, not for judging team performance.

- *Example*: During sprint reviews, use metrics to highlight achievements and areas for improvement, encouraging a constructive dialogue about performance rather than using the data for criticism.

5. **Regularly Review Metrics**: Integrate the examination of metrics into Scrum ceremonies like sprint reviews and retrospectives.

- *Example*: In each sprint review, present a summary of key metrics and their trends over time to provide a clear picture of progress and areas needing attention.

6. **Visualize Data Effectively**: Employ dashboards or information radiators to display metrics in an accessible and understandable format.

- *Example*: Use tools like digital dashboards or physical boards in the team area to display current metrics, making them visible and easily accessible to all team members and stakeholders.

7. **Adapt Metrics as Needed**: Be flexible and ready to modify your metrics approach if they are not yielding useful insights.

- *Example*: If a particular metric no longer serves its purpose or fails to provide valuable insights, reassess and adjust it, or consider replacing it with a more relevant metric.

8. **Encourage Team Reflection Based on Data**: Utilize metric data to prompt discussions about process and practice improvements.

- *Example*: During retrospectives, present specific metric trends and ask the team to reflect on what these trends indicate about their working methods, encouraging a data-driven approach to identifying improvement opportunities.

By establishing effective metrics and tracking practices, a Scrum Master can provide valuable insights into the team's progress and performance, guiding them towards continuous improvement and greater project success. These metrics are crucial for maintaining a transparent, data-driven, and improvement-oriented Scrum environment.

Advice 12: "Proactively Manage Risks, Including Opportunities, in Agile Projects"

Key Insights: Embracing Both Challenges and Opportunities in Risk Management

Effective risk management in Scrum is not only about foreseeing and mitigating potential problems but also about identifying and capitalizing on positive risks or opportunities. As a Scrum Master, your role extends to recognizing situations that could potentially bring significant benefits to the project and leveraging these opportunities. This balanced approach to risk management involves being agile and responsive to both the challenges and opportunities that arise during the project lifecycle.

Understanding Comprehensive Risk Management in Agile

- **Identify Both Threats and Opportunities**: Recognize that risks can be negative (threats) or positive (opportunities). Both types require attention and strategic planning.

- **Agile Adaptation to Risks**: Embrace an agile mindset in managing risks, adapting plans quickly to maximize opportunities and minimize threats.

- **Team Involvement in Risk Identification**: Encourage the team to be proactive in identifying both potential problems and beneficial opportunities.

Practical Tips

1. **Cultivate a Balanced Risk Perspective**: Encourage the team to view risks as both potential challenges and opportunities.

   - *Example*: During team meetings, discuss the concept of positive risks or opportunities and how they can be as impactful as negative risks, encouraging the team to shift their perspective on risk management.

2. **Regular Risk Assessment Sessions**: Conduct sessions dedicated to identifying both negative and positive risks.

   - *Example*: Schedule regular risk brainstorming sessions where the team collectively identifies potential threats and opportunities, encouraging creative thinking about what could go right as well as wrong.

3. **Evaluate and Prioritize Risks**: Assess each identified risk in terms of likelihood and potential impact, prioritizing them for action.

   - *Example*: Use a risk matrix to evaluate and categorize risks based on their severity and probability, helping the team focus on the most significant risks and opportunities.

4. **Develop Strategies for Opportunities**: Collaboratively brainstorm strategies to leverage positive risks for the project's benefit.

   - *Example*: For each positive risk identified, facilitate a discussion with the team to explore potential strategies for capitalizing on these opportunities, integrating them into the project plan where feasible.

5. **Incorporate Risks and Opportunities into Agile Ceremonies**: Address risks and opportunities during key Scrum events.

   - *Example*: Include risk review as part of the sprint planning, daily standups, and retrospectives, adjusting strategies and plans based on ongoing team feedback and project developments.

6. **Empower the Team to Pursue Opportunities**: Create an environment that supports taking calculated risks in pursuit of beneficial opportunities.

- *Example*: Encourage the team to propose and explore new ideas or approaches that align with identified opportunities, supporting them in taking well-considered risks.

7. **Maintain a Comprehensive Risk Register**: Keep an updated record of all identified risks and their associated strategies.

    - *Example*: Develop and maintain a risk register that details both threats and opportunities, along with actions taken or planned, ensuring it is regularly reviewed and updated.

8. **Communicate Openly with Stakeholders**: Keep stakeholders informed about key risks and involve them in strategic discussions.

    - *Example*: Regularly update stakeholders on the most significant risks and opportunities, seeking their input and aligning risk management strategies with broader organizational objectives and stakeholder expectations.

By managing risks comprehensively, including both threats and opportunities, a Scrum Master can guide Agile projects to not only navigate challenges effectively but also to seize potential advantages. This proactive and balanced approach to risk management is essential for fostering innovation and maximizing project success in Scrum environments.

Advice 13: "Regularly Engage in Effective Retrospectives"

Key Insights: The Value of Retrospectives in Scrum
Retrospectives are a vital component of the Scrum framework, offering regular opportunities for the team to reflect on their recent work, discuss what went well, identify areas for improvement, and plan actionable steps for future sprints. For Scrum Masters, facilitating effective retrospectives is crucial for continuous

improvement and team development. It's not just about conducting these meetings; it's about making them meaningful and productive.

Understanding the Role of Retrospectives

- **Continuous Improvement**: Retrospectives are key to the Agile principle of continuous improvement, allowing teams to evolve their practices iteratively.

- **Team Collaboration and Transparency**: These meetings foster a culture of open communication, where team members feel comfortable sharing their thoughts and feedback.

- **Action-Oriented**: Effective retrospectives focus on deriving actionable items that lead to tangible improvements in the team's processes and workflows.

Practical Tips

1. **Create a Safe Environment**: Cultivate an atmosphere where team members can share feedback openly and honestly.

   - *Example*: Begin each retrospective by reiterating the importance of a blame-free environment. Encourage constructive feedback and reassure the team that the goal is collective improvement, not individual criticism.

2. **Facilitate Balanced Participation**: Ensure that all team members have the opportunity to contribute equally to the discussion.

   - *Example*: Use round-robin techniques or anonymous feedback tools to give each team member a chance to share their thoughts. This ensures that quieter members are heard and more dominant voices do not monopolize the conversation.

3. **Focus on Actionable Outcomes**: Steer discussions toward identifying specific, achievable actions to address challenges and build on successes.

   - *Example*: After discussing what went well and what didn't, ask the team to suggest practical steps for improvement.

Document these actions and assign responsibility to ensure they are implemented.

4. **Keep it Structured Yet Flexible**: While maintaining a consistent structure, be open to adapting the format of retrospectives to suit the team's needs.

   - *Example*: Follow a structured approach like "Start, Stop, Continue," but remain open to trying new retrospective formats or techniques if the team feels the current method is no longer effective.

5. **Review Action Items in Subsequent Retrospectives**: Regularly check the progress of action items from previous retrospectives.

   - *Example*: At the beginning of each retrospective, review the action items from the last session, discuss their status, and evaluate their impact on the team's work, fostering accountability and a sense of progress.

6. **Lead by Example**: Model a reflective and open-minded attitude to encourage similar behavior from the team.

   - *Example*: Share your own reflections and learnings as a Scrum Master, showing vulnerability and openness. This sets the tone for the team and encourages them to engage more deeply in the retrospective process.

By regularly engaging in effective retrospectives and following these practical tips, a Scrum Master can significantly contribute to the team's continuous improvement, helping to refine processes, enhance collaboration, and increase the overall effectiveness of the Scrum framework.

Advice 14: "Prioritize Continuous Learning and Adaptation"

Key Insights: The Need for Ongoing Learning in Scrum

In the ever-evolving landscape of Scrum, continuous learning and adaptation are crucial for a Scrum Master. The Agile environment is characterized by rapid changes, emerging technologies, and evolving team dynamics. Staying informed, up-to-date, and adaptable is not just beneficial but necessary for effectively guiding and supporting your team.

Understanding Continuous Learning and Adaptation

- **Embrace Change**: In Agile, change is constant. Embracing change and using it as a learning opportunity is key to success.

- **Stay Informed**: Keeping up with the latest trends, tools, and methodologies in Agile and Scrum ensures that you can provide the best possible guidance to your team.

- **Adaptation to Team Needs**: Each team is unique, and what works for one may not work for another. Be ready to adapt your approach to fit the specific needs of your team.

Practical Tips

1. **Invest in Personal Development**: Dedicate regular time to your own learning and professional growth.

   - *Example*: Set aside a few hours each week to attend workshops, webinars, or online courses. Consider working towards additional certifications (see or specializations in Agile methodologies.

2. **Encourage Team Learning**: Create a culture of learning within the team, where knowledge sharing is routine and valued.

   - *Example*: Organize monthly knowledge-sharing sessions where team members can present new techniques or findings. Encourage participation in conferences or external workshops, and share the learning with the rest of the team.

3. **Stay Updated with Agile Practices**: Continuously update your knowledge of Agile practices and tools.

   - *Example*: Subscribe to Agile and Scrum-focused blogs, join online Agile communities, and participate in relevant forums or discussion groups to stay informed about the latest trends and best practices.

4. **Experiment and Reflect**: Be open to experimenting with new methods and reflect on their effectiveness.

   - *Example*: Introduce a new Agile tool or technique in your team and observe its impact. Use retrospectives as an opportunity to discuss its effectiveness and decide whether to adopt, adjust, or discard it.

5. **Share Knowledge**: Proactively share new insights and tools with your team to enhance collective learning.

   - *Example*: Share articles, case studies, or your own learnings from workshops and seminars with the team. This could be through an email newsletter, a shared digital library, or brief presentations during meetings.

6. **Solicit Feedback**: Regularly ask for feedback from your team on your methodologies and adapt based on their input.

   - *Example*: Conduct a bi-annual anonymous survey to gather feedback on your performance as a Scrum Master. Use this feedback to identify areas for improvement and to tailor your approach to better meet the needs of your team.

By prioritizing continuous learning and adaptation, a Scrum Master not only enhances their own skills and knowledge but also significantly contributes to the growth and adaptability of their Agile team. This commitment to ongoing development is essential for navigating the complexities of Agile project management and leading teams effectively.

Advice 15: "Educate and Promote Understanding of Scrum Principles"

Key Insights: Overcoming Misunderstandings of Scrum

A common challenge for Scrum Masters is addressing the lack of understanding or misconceptions about Scrum within teams, among stakeholders, and even at the management level. Misunderstandings about Scrum principles and practices can lead to ineffective implementation, resistance to Agile methodologies, and suboptimal team performance. As a Scrum Master, actively educating and clarifying Scrum principles is crucial for its successful adoption and effective practice.

Understanding the Need for Scrum Education

- **Common Misconceptions**: Recognize the common misconceptions about Scrum, such as it being a rigid methodology or just a series of meetings.

- **Tailored Communication**: Different stakeholders may require different approaches to understanding Scrum. Tailor your communication to suit their perspectives and needs.

- **Continuous Education**: Scrum is a journey, not a destination. Continuous education and reinforcement of Scrum principles are essential.

Practical Tips

1. **Organize Scrum Workshops**: Conduct regular workshops or training sessions for team members, stakeholders, and management.

   - *Example*: Plan a series of interactive workshops covering the fundamentals of Scrum, tailored to different levels of understanding and roles within the organization.

2. **Use Real-World Examples**: Clarify Scrum concepts and demonstrate its value with practical, real-world examples and case studies.

- *Example*: Share success stories or case studies from other companies or projects where Scrum principles have led to significant improvements or innovations.

3. **Tailor the Message**: Adapt your educational approach to address the specific needs and misconceptions of various groups, from team members to stakeholders.

   - *Example*: For team members, focus on how Scrum practices enhance collaboration and efficiency. For stakeholders, emphasize how Scrum can lead to better project outcomes and ROI.

4. **Encourage Hands-On Learning**: Provide opportunities for experiential learning through simulations or pilot projects.

   - *Example*: Organize a mock Scrum project, allowing participants to engage in roles like Product Owner, Scrum Master, and team members, to experience Scrum dynamics firsthand.

5. **Leverage Agile Coaches or Experts**: Involve Agile coaches or external experts to lend additional perspectives and credibility to your educational efforts.

   - *Example*: Invite an experienced Agile coach for a Q&A session or a specialized workshop to address advanced Scrum topics or challenges.

6. **Develop Educational Resources**: Create a resource library with articles, videos, and guides for ongoing self-learning.

   - *Example*: Compile a digital repository of Scrum resources accessible to all team members, with materials ranging from introductory articles to in-depth guides.

7. **Reinforce Learning in Agile Ceremonies**: Utilize Agile ceremonies like sprint reviews and retrospectives to discuss and reinforce Scrum principles.

- *Example*: During retrospectives, relate team experiences and challenges back to Scrum principles, discussing how adherence to these principles could improve future sprints.

8. **Promote Open Dialogue**: Foster an environment where questions and discussions about Scrum are encouraged in team meetings.

   - *Example*: Allocate time in team meetings for an open forum where team members can ask questions or share experiences related to Scrum, facilitating a culture of continuous learning and open communication.

By actively educating and promoting a thorough understanding of Scrum principles, a Scrum Master can effectively address misconceptions and resistance, paving the way for a more cohesive and productive adoption of Agile methodologies. This educational role is crucial for fostering a culture that embraces Scrum and its benefits.

Advice 16: "Effectively Manage Stakeholder Engagement"

Key Insights: The Importance of Stakeholder Engagement in Scrum

In Scrum, effective stakeholder engagement is vital. Stakeholders can include anyone from business executives and customers to end users who have a vested interest in the project's outcome. As a Scrum Master, actively managing stakeholder engagement is crucial for ensuring that the team receives the necessary support, feedback, and resources. Proper stakeholder engagement leads to more aligned expectations, better decision-making, and enhanced project value.

Understanding Stakeholder Engagement in Agile

- **Balancing Input and Team Autonomy**: It's important to balance stakeholder input with maintaining the team's autonomy and adherence to Agile principles.

- **Regular Communication**: Keeping stakeholders informed and involved in a way that is consistent with Agile practices.

- **Feedback Integration**: Efficiently integrating stakeholder feedback into the development process to enhance product value.

Practical Tips

1. **Identify and Analyze Stakeholders**: Understand who the stakeholders are, their interests in the project, and their level of influence.

   - *Example*: Create a stakeholder map to identify all relevant stakeholders, categorize them based on their interest and influence, and develop tailored strategies for engaging each group effectively.

2. **Facilitate Regular Updates**: Keep stakeholders informed about the project's progress through regular communications.

   - *Example*: Schedule monthly stakeholder update meetings or circulate a regular newsletter summarizing the project's progress, key achievements, and upcoming goals.

3. **Encourage Stakeholder Participation**: Invite stakeholders to participate in specific Agile ceremonies where their input can be most valuable.

   - *Example*: Encourage stakeholders to attend sprint review meetings, where they can see the work completed during the sprint and provide immediate feedback.

4. **Manage Expectations**: Clearly communicate the Agile process to stakeholders, setting realistic expectations for project deliverables and timelines.

- *Example*: Conduct an initial briefing session for stakeholders to explain the iterative nature of Agile development, the concept of MVP (Minimum Viable Product), and how this approach benefits the project.

5. **Seek Feedback Constructively**: Proactively solicit and facilitate the collection of constructive feedback from stakeholders.

   - *Example*: Create a structured feedback form or system that stakeholders can use to provide their input after each sprint review, focusing on constructive and actionable insights.

6. **Advocate for the Team**: Represent the team's interests and constraints in discussions with stakeholders, ensuring mutual understanding and support.

   - *Example*: During stakeholder meetings, clearly articulate the team's capabilities, constraints, and needs, and advocate for conditions that enable the team to work effectively.

7. **Collaborate on Prioritization**: Work with the Product Owner and stakeholders to align the team's work with stakeholder priorities, while adhering to Agile values.

   - *Example*: Facilitate prioritization sessions with the Product Owner and key stakeholders to align the product backlog with stakeholder needs, ensuring that prioritization decisions are transparent and collaborative.

By effectively managing stakeholder engagement, a Scrum Master can bridge the gap between the team and its stakeholders, ensuring a smoother workflow, clearer communication, and a product that meets or exceeds stakeholder expectations. This role is crucial in maximizing the value delivered by the Agile team and maintaining a harmonious and productive relationship with stakeholders.

Advice 17: "Navigate Team Conflicts with Tact and Empathy"

Key Insights: The Scrum Master's Role in Conflict Management

Conflict is a natural part of any team dynamic, especially in high-pressure environments like Scrum. As a Scrum Master, one of your roles is to help navigate and resolve conflicts within the team. Effective conflict management is crucial not only for maintaining a harmonious team environment but also for fostering trust, collaboration, and growth. The way conflicts are managed can significantly impact team morale and productivity.

Understanding Conflict Management in Agile

- **Early Intervention**: Addressing conflicts early on before they escalate into larger issues.

- **Empathy and Understanding**: Approaching conflicts with empathy, aiming to understand all perspectives.

- **Facilitating Constructive Dialogue**: Creating a safe space for open and honest communication where team members can express their concerns and work towards resolution.

Practical Tips

1. **Recognize Signs of Conflict**: Be vigilant and proactive in identifying early indicators of team conflicts.

   - *Example*: Pay attention to changes in team interactions, such as increased disagreements, withdrawal of team members, or a drop in collaboration. Address these signs early through individual discussions or team meetings.

2. **Encourage Open Communication**: Create a safe space for team members to express their concerns and opinions openly and respectfully.

   - *Example*: During team meetings, allocate time for team members to voice any concerns or issues they may have. Emphasize the importance of respectful and constructive communication.

3. **Remain Neutral and Unbiased**: In conflict situations, maintain an impartial stance and focus on understanding the underlying causes.

   - *Example*: When mediating conflicts, listen to all sides without showing bias. Ask neutral questions that help uncover the root causes of the conflict, rather than placing blame.

4. **Facilitate Problem-Solving Sessions**: Conduct sessions specifically aimed at resolving conflicts, guiding the team in finding solutions that are acceptable to all parties.

   - *Example*: Organize a dedicated meeting to address the conflict, using structured problem-solving techniques like brainstorming or root cause analysis to guide the discussion towards resolution.

5. **Use Active Listening Skills**: Practice active listening to ensure all parties feel heard and understood in a conflict situation.

   - *Example*: In conflict discussions, repeat back what you've heard to confirm understanding, and ask clarifying questions. This approach helps to ensure that all viewpoints are accurately represented and understood.

6. **Promote Empathy and Understanding**: Encourage team members to consider and understand each other's perspectives.

   - *Example*: Facilitate exercises or discussions that help team members step into each other's shoes, such as role reversal exercises, to foster empathy and understanding.

7. **Provide Training and Resources**: If conflicts are a recurring issue, consider offering training in conflict resolution and communication skills.

   - *Example*: Arrange workshops or training sessions on effective communication, conflict resolution strategies, or emotional intelligence to equip team members with the skills to manage conflicts more effectively.

8. **Seek External Help When Necessary**: If conflicts are complex or persistent, do not hesitate to seek assistance from HR professionals or conflict resolution experts.

- *Example*: In cases where team conflicts are deeply rooted or disruptive, engage with HR or professional mediators to facilitate resolution, ensuring that the process is handled professionally and effectively.

By adeptly navigating team conflicts, a Scrum Master plays a key role in maintaining a positive and productive team environment. Effective conflict management not only resolves immediate disagreements but also strengthens the team's ability to handle future challenges collaboratively and constructively.

Advice 18: "Navigate Global Virtual Team Dynamics"

Key Insights: Challenges of Global Virtual Teams in Scrum

Managing a global virtual team presents unique challenges for a Scrum Master, especially in the context of Scrum. These challenges include time zone differences, cultural diversity, communication barriers, and the lack of face-to-face interaction. As a Scrum Master for such a team, it's essential to develop strategies to effectively navigate these complexities, ensuring cohesive and efficient team collaboration across borders.

Understanding Global Virtual Team Dynamics

- **Cultural Sensitivity**: Being aware of and respectful towards the cultural differences within the team.

- **Communication Strategies**: Adapting communication methods to suit a virtual, globally dispersed team.

- **Building Trust Remotely**: Establishing trust in a virtual environment, where face-to-face interactions are limited.

Practical Tips

1. **Establish Clear Communication Protocols**: Set up structured communication channels and guidelines that accommodate different time zones and working preferences.

   - *Example*: Create a communication plan that specifies the preferred channels (e.g., email, chat, video calls) for different types of communication and establishes guidelines for response times, considering the various time zones of team members.

2. **Leverage Technology Effectively**: Use collaboration and communication tools that support remote teamwork efficiently.

   - *Example*: Implement collaborative tools such as Slack for instant messaging, Zoom for video conferencing, and Trello or Jira for project management. Ensure that all team members are trained and comfortable with these tools.

3. **Schedule Inclusive Meetings**: Organize meetings at times that accommodate all team members, and consider rotating meeting times.

   - *Example*: Plan meetings using a schedule that rotates the meeting time, so the inconvenience of very early or late meetings is shared fairly among all team members.

4. **Foster Cultural Awareness**: Promote an understanding of diverse cultural backgrounds within the team.

   - *Example*: Host regular sessions where team members can share aspects of their culture or working style. This can include informal virtual coffee breaks or cultural awareness workshops.

5. **Build Strong Relationships**: Encourage team bonding and relationship-building despite the lack of physical presence.

   - *Example*: Arrange virtual team-building activities, such as online games or virtual lunch meetings, to create opportunities for informal interaction and rapport building.

6. **Regular Check-ins and Support**: Hold consistent one-on-one meetings with team members for personalized support and to address any issues.

   - *Example*: Schedule regular virtual check-ins with each team member to discuss their progress, challenges, and any support they may need, ensuring these sessions are tailored to their time zone and availability.

7. **Adapt Agile Practices**: Modify Agile ceremonies and practices to suit a virtual environment without losing their effectiveness.

   - *Example*: Conduct shorter, more focused daily stand-ups via video call and utilize digital boards for sprint planning and retrospectives to maintain engagement and participation from remote team members.

By effectively navigating the dynamics of global virtual teams, a Scrum Master can foster a productive, collaborative, and culturally sensitive environment. This approach is key to overcoming the inherent challenges of remote teamwork and ensuring the success of Agile projects in a global virtual context.

Advice 19: "Address Aggression and Cyber Aggression"

Key Insights: The Scrum Master's Role in Managing Workplace Aggression

As a Scrum Master, it's crucial to address any form of aggression, including bullying, harassment, sexual harassment, and incivility, whether it occurs in-person or virtually (cyber aggression). These behaviors can significantly harm team morale, trust, and productivity. Handling such situations with sensitivity, confidentiality, and firmness is vital for maintaining a safe and respectful team environment.

Understanding Workplace Aggression

- **Zero Tolerance Policy**: Adopting a clear stance that any form of aggression or harassment is unacceptable.

- **Creating a Safe Environment**: Ensuring that team members feel safe to report incidents without fear of retaliation or judgment.

- **Confidentiality and Sensitivity**: Handling all reports and incidents with utmost confidentiality and sensitivity.

Practical Tips

1. **Establish Clear Guidelines**: Implement and communicate explicit guidelines about workplace behavior and the consequences of aggression or harassment.

   - *Example*: Develop a team charter or code of conduct that clearly defines acceptable behaviors and the procedures for addressing misconduct. Regularly review and discuss these guidelines with the team to ensure understanding and compliance.

2. **Provide Training**: Offer regular training sessions on appropriate workplace behaviors, including recognizing and reporting harassment and aggression.

   - *Example*: Arrange annual training workshops on topics like workplace harassment, cyberbullying, and creating a respectful work environment. These sessions should be mandatory for all team members.

3. **Encourage Reporting**: Foster a safe environment where team members feel confident to report any incidents of aggression, assuring them of confidentiality and protection from retaliation.

   - *Example*: Set up an anonymous reporting system or designate a neutral person (such as an HR representative) whom team members can approach to report concerns confidentially.

4. **Respond Promptly and Appropriately**: Act swiftly and in line with organizational protocols upon receiving reports of aggression or harassment.

   - *Example*: When an incident is reported, immediately initiate the organization's established procedure for investigating and addressing such matters, ensuring fairness and confidentiality throughout the process.

5. **Support Affected Individuals**: Provide support to team members who have been affected by aggression or harassment.

   - *Example*: Offer access to counseling services or employee assistance programs, and if necessary, adjust team dynamics or project assignments temporarily to protect the affected individual.

6. **Monitor Team Interactions**: Remain observant of team interactions, particularly in virtual settings where cyber aggression may be less obvious.

   - *Example*: In virtual meetings and communications, watch for signs of negative behavior such as exclusion, derogatory comments, or overbearing behavior, and address them proactively.

7. **Collaborate with HR and Management**: Work closely with HR and upper management to handle incidents of aggression effectively.

   - *Example*: In cases of reported aggression, partner with HR to ensure that the issue is handled appropriately and in accordance with company policies and legal requirements.

8. **Foster a Culture of Respect**: Continually promote and model respect, empathy, and professionalism within the team.

   - *Example*: Lead by example in demonstrating respectful behavior and openly acknowledge and praise positive team interactions that exemplify the desired culture. Regularly remind the team of the value of a respectful and inclusive work environment.

By effectively addressing aggression and cyber aggression, a Scrum Master plays a critical role in safeguarding the team's well-being and maintaining a healthy, respectful, and productive work environment. This responsibility is key to fostering a culture of trust and collaboration in any Agile team.

Advice 20: "Foster Motivation and Engagement in Scrum Teams"

Key Insights: Enhancing Team Motivation and Engagement

Maintaining high levels of motivation and engagement is essential for the success and health of a Scrum team. As a Scrum Master, fostering a culture that values continuous learning, recognizes achievements, and celebrates successes is key. Motivated and engaged teams are more productive, more collaborative, and more likely to produce high-quality results.

Understanding Motivation in Scrum

- **Intrinsic Motivation**: Recognize that motivation often comes from within the team – their passion for the work, their commitment to the project's goals, and their desire to succeed as a team.

- **Creating a Positive Environment**: A positive, supportive environment fosters engagement and motivation.

- **Recognition and Reward**: Regularly acknowledging and celebrating achievements can greatly enhance team morale and motivation.

Practical Tips

1. **Set Clear and Achievable Goals**: Collaborate with the team to establish clear, realistic goals that align with project objectives and team capabilities.

- *Example*: During sprint planning, facilitate a goal-setting session where team members contribute to defining achievable sprint goals, ensuring these goals are challenging yet attainable and clearly understood by all.

2. **Encourage Continuous Learning**: Promote a culture of growth and continuous improvement within the team.

   - *Example*: Encourage team members to pursue relevant training or workshops. Allocate time during sprints for learning activities or knowledge-sharing sessions where team members can learn from each other.

3. **Recognize Individual and Team Achievements**: Regularly acknowledge both individual efforts and team successes.

   - *Example*: Give shout-outs during team meetings for individual contributions or create a team 'kudos' board where team members can recognize each other's achievements.

4. **Celebrate Milestones**: Take time to celebrate significant achievements and milestones.

   - *Example*: Organize a virtual celebration or team lunch after the completion of a major project phase or the successful launch of a feature, acknowledging the team's hard work and success.

5. **Facilitate Team Bonding**: Arrange activities that not only are enjoyable but also strengthen team cohesion.

   - *Example*: Plan periodic team-building activities, like virtual escape rooms or online game sessions, which can help in building stronger relationships among team members.

6. **Provide Constructive Feedback**: Offer feedback that is actionable and focused on helping team members grow and improve.

- *Example*: During one-on-one meetings, provide specific, constructive feedback that focuses on behaviors or skills the team member can develop, coupled with recognition of their strengths.

7. **Empower Team Members**: Grant team members autonomy in their tasks and decision-making, demonstrating trust in their abilities.

   - *Example*: Allow team members to self-organize and make decisions about their work, providing guidance and support only when necessary.

8. **Monitor Workload to Prevent Burnout**: Keep a close watch on the team's workload to ensure it is sustainable.

   - *Example*: Regularly check in with team members about their workload and stress levels, and be prepared to adjust assignments or timelines to prevent burnout.

By actively working to maintain motivation and engagement, a Scrum Master can help ensure that the team not only performs well but also enjoys the process. A motivated and engaged team is more resilient, collaborative, and effective, which is essential in the dynamic and challenging world of Scrum.

Advice 21: "Balance Multiple Teams Effectively as a Scrum Master"

Key Insights: Navigating the Challenges of Managing Multiple Teams

For Scrum Masters who are responsible for more than one team, the challenge lies in balancing time and attention effectively. Each team has its unique dynamics, needs, and challenges, and providing adequate support to all is crucial. This balancing act requires strategic planning, excellent communication skills, and the ability to prioritize effectively without compromising the quality of support provided to each team.

Understanding the Management of Multiple Teams

- **Individual Team Needs**: Recognize that each team has its own set of needs, goals, and working styles.

- **Effective Prioritization**: Learn to prioritize tasks and allocate your time based on the urgency and impact on each team.

- **Consistency in Scrum Practices**: Ensure that Scrum practices are consistently applied across all teams, while being adaptable to each team's specific context.

Practical Tips

1. **Know Each Team Well**: Spend time understanding the unique dynamics, strengths, weaknesses, and needs of each team you manage.

   - *Example*: Regularly schedule time with each team to observe their interactions, understand their project challenges, and get to know each team member's strengths and areas for growth.

2. **Set Clear Boundaries and Expectations**: Clearly communicate your availability to each team and set realistic expectations regarding how and when you can be reached.

   - *Example*: Inform each team of your schedule, specifying the times you are dedicated to them and establishing guidelines for how they can reach you outside of these times.

3. **Prioritize Based on Need and Impact**: Evaluate the current needs of each team and prioritize your time and attention based on urgency and importance.

   - *Example*: If one team is approaching a critical project deadline while another is in a more stable phase, allocate more time to the team in the critical phase.

4. **Use Time Management Tools**: Implement scheduling tools and task lists to efficiently manage and allocate your time among the teams.

- *Example*: Use digital calendars to block out dedicated times for each team and employ task management tools to keep track of your commitments and responsibilities for each group.

5. **Delegate and Empower**: Delegate appropriate responsibilities within teams and empower team members to take on more significant roles.

   - *Example*: Identify team members who can handle certain responsibilities, such as facilitating a daily standup or leading a retrospective, to reduce your direct involvement without compromising the team's progress.

6. **Regular Check-ins**: Schedule consistent check-ins with each team to stay informed about their progress and address issues promptly.

   - *Example*: Arrange weekly or bi-weekly one-on-one meetings with team leads or members to discuss their progress, challenges, and any support they might need.

7. **Foster Inter-Team Communication**: Promote communication and collaboration between your teams, especially if their projects are interrelated or they have shared skills.

   - *Example*: Organize joint meetings or knowledge-sharing sessions between teams to facilitate the exchange of ideas and experiences, enhancing collaboration and learning.

8. **Reflect and Adjust**: Regularly evaluate how effectively you're managing multiple teams and be open to adjusting your approach based on feedback and changing needs.

   - *Example*: Periodically ask for feedback from each team on your management style and effectiveness. Reflect on this feedback and adjust your approach to better support each team's unique needs.

By effectively balancing the needs of multiple teams, a Scrum Master can ensure that each team receives the necessary support and guidance, leading to successful outcomes for all. This balance is key to fulfilling the multifaceted role of a Scrum Master in a dynamic and complex Agile environment.

Advice 22: "Understand and Align with Scaled Agile Frameworks"

Key Insights: Navigating Scaled Agile Frameworks as a Scrum Master

In environments where Agile methodologies are scaled to accommodate larger teams and more complex projects, understanding and aligning with scaled Agile frameworks becomes essential for a Scrum Master. Scaled Agile Frameworks like SAFe (Scaled Agile Framework), LeSS (Large-Scale Scrum), and Scrum of Scrums are designed to facilitate Agile practices in larger organizations. As a Scrum Master, comprehending these frameworks and their implications on your role is crucial for effectively managing larger teams and ensuring alignment with the broader organizational goals.

Understanding Scaled Agile Frameworks

- **Frameworks Overview**: Familiarize yourself with the principles, structures, and practices of various scaled Agile frameworks.

- **Integration with Organizational Goals**: Understand how these frameworks align Agile teams with the overall strategic objectives of the organization.

- **Facilitating Collaboration Across Teams**: In scaled environments, collaboration extends beyond individual teams to include cross-team coordination and alignment.

Practical Tips

1. **Educate Yourself on Scaled Agile Frameworks**: Deepen your knowledge of various scaled Agile frameworks through self-study and professional development.

- *Example*: Enroll in certification courses or attend workshops on SAFe, LeSS, or other scaled Agile frameworks. Read official guides and books, and stay updated with the latest developments in these frameworks.

2. **Understand Your Role within the Framework**: Grasp how the Scrum Master role evolves within a scaled Agile setting, including any additional responsibilities.

   - *Example*: Study case studies or seek mentorship to understand the nuances of the Scrum Master role in a scaled environment, such as your involvement in cross-team coordination and enterprise-level planning.

3. **Facilitate Effective Communication Across Teams**: Ensure that there is clear, effective communication between different Scrum teams, particularly around dependencies and shared objectives.

   - *Example*: Establish regular sync-up meetings or communication channels where Scrum teams can discuss interdependencies, share updates, and collaborate on solutions.

4. **Encourage Consistency in Agile Practices**: Advocate for uniformity in Agile practices across all teams within the scaled framework to maintain coherence and efficiency.

   - *Example*: Work with other Scrum Masters and Agile Coaches to develop a shared understanding and consistent application of Agile principles and practices across teams.

5. **Participate in Scaled Planning Meetings**: Actively contribute to large-scale planning sessions, bringing your unique perspective as a Scrum Master.

   - *Example*: Play an active role in Program Increment (PI) Planning sessions in SAFe or similar events in other frameworks, providing insights into team capacities and impediments.

6. **Collaborate with Other Scrum Masters and Agile Coaches**: Engage with fellow Scrum Masters and Agile Coaches to exchange knowledge and strategies.

- *Example*: Join a community of practice for Scrum Masters within your organization or participate in external Agile forums to discuss challenges and share experiences in a scaled Agile environment.

By understanding and aligning with scaled Agile frameworks, a Scrum Master can effectively contribute to the success of Agile practices on a larger scale, ensuring that their team's efforts are in sync with the broader organizational objectives. This understanding is pivotal for thriving in environments where Agile is implemented at scale.

Advice 23: "Integrate DevOps Practices into Agile Teams"

Key Insights: The Synergy of DevOps and Scrum

For Scrum Masters, understanding and integrating DevOps practices into Agile teams is increasingly important. DevOps, a set of practices that combines software development (Dev) and IT operations (Ops), aims to shorten the development lifecycle and provide continuous delivery with high software quality. This integration is crucial in today's fast-paced software development environment, where the alignment of development and operations is key to achieving agility and efficiency.

Understanding the Role of DevOps in Agile

- **Enhanced Collaboration**: DevOps fosters a culture of collaboration between developers and operations teams, breaking down silos and improving efficiency.

- **Continuous Improvement**: Similar to Agile, DevOps emphasizes continuous improvement, particularly in the areas of software delivery and quality.

- **Rapid Feedback Loops**: DevOps practices enable quicker feedback loops, ensuring that any issues in the software development lifecycle are addressed swiftly.

Practical Tips

1. **Familiarize with DevOps Principles**: Deepen your understanding of DevOps principles and practices, focusing on how they impact software development and operations.

   - *Example*: Enroll in online courses, attend workshops, or participate in webinars focused on DevOps methodologies. Read books and articles to stay updated on the latest DevOps trends and best practices.

2. **Promote a Collaborative Culture**: Encourage and facilitate collaboration between the development and operations teams.

   - *Example*: Organize joint meetings between developers and operations staff to discuss common goals, share challenges, and brainstorm solutions that benefit the entire software lifecycle.

3. **Advocate for Automation**: Support the implementation of automation in testing, deployment, and monitoring processes.

   - *Example*: Encourage the team to adopt tools for automated testing and continuous integration, demonstrating how automation can streamline processes and enhance efficiency.

4. **Implement Continuous Integration/Continuous Delivery (CI/CD)**: Encourage the use of CI/CD pipelines to facilitate frequent and reliable code changes.

   - *Example*: Work with the team to set up and optimize CI/CD pipelines, ensuring that they are integrated into the team's daily development practices and align with Agile's iterative approach.

5. **Incorporate DevOps into Retrospectives**: Discuss the integration and impact of DevOps practices in retrospectives to identify improvement areas.

   - *Example*: During retrospectives, review how effectively the team is integrating DevOps practices and identify any obstacles they face, discussing ways to overcome them.

6. **Build Cross-Functional Awareness**: Conduct sessions where team members can learn about both development and operations, enhancing mutual understanding.

   - *Example*: Facilitate knowledge-sharing sessions or "day in the life" experiences where team members can shadow colleagues in different roles, fostering a better understanding of each other's responsibilities and challenges.

By integrating DevOps practices into Agile teams, a Scrum Master can significantly contribute to enhancing the team's efficiency, collaboration, and ability to deliver high-quality software rapidly. This integration is a strategic move towards building more robust, responsive, and effective Agile teams in the realm of software development.

Final Reflections: Embracing the Agile Journey

As we reach the conclusion, it's important to pause and reflect on the journey we've traversed together. Through the 23 pieces of advice presented in this book, we've explored the multifaceted role of the Scrum Master and the myriad challenges and opportunities encountered in Agile environments.

Key Takeaways

- **Empowerment and Flexibility**: The essence of Agile and Scrum lies in empowering teams, fostering flexibility, and embracing change. As Scrum Masters, your role is pivotal in nurturing these principles.

- **Continuous Learning and Adaptation**: The Agile journey is one of continual learning and adaptation. Each piece of advice underscores the importance of staying open, curious, and adaptable to the evolving dynamics of Agile project management.

- **Collaboration and Communication**: Effective collaboration and clear communication are the cornerstones of successful Agile teams. The Scrum Master's role in facilitating these aspects cannot be overstated.

- **Servant Leadership**: Embodying servant leadership, focusing on serving the team rather than leading from the front, is crucial in guiding teams toward self-organization and excellence.

Moving Forward

As you continue your journey as a Scrum Master, remember that each project, each team, and each challenge is a unique opportunity for growth and improvement. The principles and practices outlined in this book are not just guidelines but tools for you to adapt and apply in your own context.

The Agile Mindset

Above all, embrace the Agile mindset. Be receptive to feedback, willing to experiment, and ready to adapt. Your journey as a Scrum Master is not just about managing projects but about leading teams to achieve their best, fostering innovation, and delivering value.

Your Role in the Agile Landscape

As Agile methodologies continue to evolve and adapt to the changing landscapes of technology and business, your role as a Scrum Master will be instrumental in shaping the future of project management. You are not just a part of the Agile journey; you are a driving force behind its success.

In Closing

May this book serve as a compass on your Agile journey, guiding you through the challenges and celebrating the triumphs. The path of Agile is continuous, and each step forward is a step towards mastery, innovation, and collaborative success.

Certifications for Current and Aspiring Scrum Masters

1. **Certified ScrumMaster (CSM)** by Scrum Alliance

   - https://www.scrumalliance.org/get-certified/scrum-master-track/certified-scrummaster

   - This certification provides a comprehensive understanding of Scrum methodology, focusing on the role of a Scrum Master. It equips individuals with the knowledge and skills needed to facilitate Scrum practices effectively and to lead Agile teams.

   - No experience is required.

2. **Advanced Certified ScrumMaster (A-CSM)** by Scrum Alliance

   - https://www.scrumalliance.org/get-certified/scrum-master-track/advanced-certified-scrummaster

   - This is a step beyond the basic CSM certification. It helps Scrum Masters develop advanced facilitation and coaching skills, crucial for tackling complex team dynamics and enhancing team performance.

   - At least one year of year of work experience specific to the role of ScrumMaster (within the past five years).

3. **Certified Scrum Professional - ScrumMaster (CSP-SM)** by Scrum Alliance

   - https://www.scrumalliance.org/get-certified/scrum-master-track/certified-scrum-professional-scrummaster

- This is a more advanced level than the A-CSM certification. It's designed for Scrum Masters who have significant experience in the field and are looking to elevate their expertise to a higher level. Achieving the CSP-SM certification can open doors to more advanced and specialized roles in Agile and Scrum environments, marking the holder as a highly skilled and knowledgeable Scrum Master.

- At least two years of work experience specific to the role of ScrumMaster (within the past five years).

Scrum Alliance offers 15 more certifications. Visit https://www.scrumalliance.org/get-certified for more information.

4. **Professional Scrum Master (PSM)** by Scrum.org

- https://www.scrum.org/assessments/professional-scrum-master-i-certification

- PSM certifications, especially PSM I, II, and III, offer deep insights into Scrum practices and the principles underlying Agile methodologies. They focus on practical application, enhancing a Scrum Master's ability to implement Scrum in various environments.

    i. PSM I: No formal experience requirements.

    ii. PSM II: While there are no strict prerequisites in terms of years of experience, it is intended for experienced Scrum Masters.

    iii. PSM III: It is expected that candidates have significant experience as a Scrum Master, as it involves a deeper understanding of the principles and practices of Scrum and the ability to apply them in complex, real-world situations.

Scrum.org offers 10 more certifications. Visit https://www.scrum.org/professional-scrum-certifications for more information.

5. **SAFe® Scrum Master** by Scaled Agile

- https://scaledagile.com/training/safe-scrum-master/

- This certification is focused on integrating Scrum practices within the Scaled Agile Framework (SAFe). It's designed for individuals who wish to take on the role of Scrum Master in a SAFe environment.

- While specific experience requirements may vary, having a background in Scrum or Agile practices can be beneficial.

6. **SAFe® Advanced Scrum Master** by Scaled Agile

- https://scaledagile.com/training/safe-advanced-scrum-master/

- It is designed for current Scrum Masters who seek to enhance their skills in facilitating Agile teams, managing Agile programs, and implementing the SAFe.

- Having a foundational certification like the SAFe Scrum Master (SSM) is recommended or required.

Scaled Agile offers 11 more certifications. Visit https://scaledagile.com/calendar/which-course-is-right-for-you/ for more information.

7. **Disciplined Agile® Scrum Master (DASM)** Certification by PMI

- https://www.pmi.org/certifications/agile-certifications/disciplined-agile-scrum-master-dasm

- It is designed for individuals seeking to understand and apply Disciplined Agile (DA) practices. It is suitable for those new to Agile or those familiar with other Agile approaches like Scrum, Lean, or Kanban.

- There is no experience requirement.

8. **Disciplined Agile® Senior Scrum Master (DASSM)** Certification by PMI

- https://www.pmi.org/certifications/agile-certifications/disciplined-agile-senior-scrum-master-dassm

- DASSM teaches experienced agile practitioners how to use the Disciplined Agile tool kit to optimize how teams work, work with allies within their organization, and solve a variety of advanced problems.

- Two years of experience working in an agile team, ideally in a leadership role such as Disciplined Agile scrum master, scrum master, product owner, or architecture owner.

PMI (Project Management Institute) offers three more certifications. Visit https://www.pmi.org/certifications/agile-certifications for more information.